Samuel French Acting Edition

The Property Known as Garland

by Billy Van Zandt

SAMUELFRENCH.COM   SAMUELFRENCH.CO.UK

Copyright © 2007 by William Van Zandt Living Trust
All Rights Reserved

THE PROPERTY KNOWN AS GARLAND is fully protected under the copyright laws of the United States of America, the British Commonwealth, including Canada, and all other countries of the Copyright Union. All rights, including professional and amateur stage productions, recitation, lecturing, public reading, motion picture, radio broadcasting, television and the rights of translation into foreign languages are strictly reserved.

ISBN 978-0-573-64239-5

www.SamuelFrench.com
www.SamuelFrench.co.uk

For Production Enquiries

United States and Canada
Info@SamuelFrench.com
1-866-598-8449

United Kingdom and Europe
Plays@SamuelFrench.co.uk
020-7255-4302

Each title is subject to availability from Samuel French, depending upon country of performance. Please be aware that *THE PROPERTY KNOWN AS GARLAND* may not be licensed by Samuel French in your territory. Professional and amateur producers should contact the nearest Samuel French office or licensing partner to verify availability.

CAUTION: Professional and amateur producers are hereby warned that *THE PROPERTY KNOWN AS GARLAND* is subject to a licensing fee. Publication of this play(s) does not imply availability for performance. Both amateurs and professionals considering a production are strongly advised to apply to Samuel French before starting rehearsals, advertising, or booking a theatre. A licensing fee must be paid whether the title(s) is presented for charity or gain and whether or not admission is charged. Professional/Stock licensing fees are quoted upon application to Samuel French.

No one shall make any changes in this title(s) for the purpose of production. No part of this book may be reproduced, stored in a retrieval system, or transmitted in any form, by any means, now known or yet to be invented, including mechanical, electronic, photocopying, recording, videotaping, or otherwise, without the prior written permission of the publisher. No one shall upload this title(s), or part of this title(s), to any social media websites.

For all enquiries regarding motion picture, television, and other media rights, please contact Samuel French.

MUSIC USE NOTE

Licensees are solely responsible for obtaining formal written permission from copyright owners to use copyrighted music in the performance of this play and are strongly cautioned to do so. If no such permission is obtained by the licensee, then the licensee must use only original music that the licensee owns and controls. Licensees are solely responsible and liable for all music clearances and shall indemnify the copyright owners of the play(s) and their licensing agent, Samuel French, against any costs, expenses, losses and liabilities arising from the use of music by licensees. Please contact the appropriate music licensing authority in your territory for the rights to any incidental music.

IMPORTANT BILLING AND CREDIT REQUIREMENTS

If you have obtained performance rights to this title, please refer to your licensing agreement for important billing and credit requirements.

MUSIC CREDITS FOR
THE PROPERTY KNOWN AS GARLAND

THE PROPERTY KNOWN AS GARLAND includes the music publishing rights to the following songs. Music credits *must* be given to the composers and publishers for all productions.

"Over the Rainbow"
Written by E.Y. Harburg and Harold Arlen
Published by EMI Feist Catalog Inc.

"The Trolley Song"
Written by Hugh Martin and Ralph Blaine
Published by EMI Feist Catalog Inc.

"Cry"
Written by Churchill Kohlman
Used by permission of Shapiro, Bernstein & Co., Inc.
All rights reserved. International copyright secured.

"Swanee" and "The Land of Let's Pretend" are in the Public Domain in the United States and may be used without permission unless you are using them outside the U.S.

Rights to the play do NOT include:
"Zing Went the Strings of My Heart"
Written by James Hanley
Published by Warner Bros., Inc.
Producers must make separate arrangements with the publisher for the use of this song.

THE PROPERTY KNOWN AS GARLAND opened Off-Broadway at the Actors Playhouse on Thursday March 23, 2006. It was produced by Billy Van Zandt, Barry Krost, Sally V. Winters, Mark Fleming and Jane Milmore. It was directed by Glenn Casale with the following cast:

JUDY GARLAND	Adrienne Barbeau
ED	Kerby Joe Grubb
Standby for ED	Jonathan E. Schultz

Set Design by Charlie Smith
Lighting Design by Richard Winkler
Costume Design by Cynthia Nordstrom
Sound Design by Jill BC DuBoff
Wig Design by David H. Lawrence
Makeup Design by Stacey Panepinto
Production Stage Manager: Thom Schilling
Assistant Stage Manager: Jonathan E. Schultz
General Management by 321 Theatrical Management
Press Representative: Keith Sherman & Associates
Marketing by HHC Marketing
Advertising by Eliran Murphy Group
Legal Services by Mark Sendroff and Associates
Production Photography by Carol Rosegg
Poster Photography by Danny Sanchez
Company Manager: Lauren Yates

(Curtain rises on the star dressing room of the Falconre Centre, Copenhagen, Denmark, March 25, 1969. A dressing table and chair are D.S.C. A club chair and side table sit S.L. A dressing screen and wardrobe rack sit U.S.R. The chaise is D.S.R. An exit to the restroom is S.R. The dressing room door to the stage is U.S.C. Wine bottles litter the room. There is a knock at the door.)

ED. *(Off)* Miss Garland? One hour, Miss Garland.

(ED, a good-looking blonde Assistant Stage Manager of nineteen, enters. We hear the sounds of opening act Johnnie Ray's audience/show outside the open door.)

ED. Miss Garland? Miss Garland? One hour, Miss Garland.

(ED flips on the lights, seeing the wine bottles. The great JUDY GARLAND enters from the restroom, bombed, slurring, and out of control. She holds a half-filled wine glass.)

JUDY. Who the fuck are you?

(She stumbles. ED catches her.)

ED. Omigod. Ed.
JUDY. Hello, Ed. *(Staring up into his eyes.)* How old are you?

ED. Nineteen.
JUDY. Nineteen? Nobody's nineteen anymore. Where's Mickey?
ED. I don't know who you mean. Mickey Rooney? Where's Mickey Rooney?
JUDY. How the hell would I know where Mickey Rooney is? Try the track. My husband—the new one.
ED. I'm not sure, Ma'am.
JUDY. Well, you find him and tell him I'm not going on tonight. I just don't feel like it. *(Ed reacts to her casualness.)* Just give them their money back and tell them to come back tomorrow.
ED. You're not here tomorrow. Miss Garland, this is the last night of your tour. And we're sold out. You're sold out.
JUDY. I always sell out! Who do you think I am, Kate Fucking Smith? *(Laughs. JUDY crosses to the chaise and flops down.)* Wouldn't you love to see *that* on a marquee?
ED. Oh, boy. Johnnie Ray's already on.
JUDY. Who?
ED. Johnnie Ray. Johnnie Ray! Your opening act.
JUDY. He's a drunk.

(JUDY takes a big sip of wine.)

ED. Yes. But...he's on. And it's packed out there. Some peoples have been waiting—
JUDY. I don't care if they're turning to stone.
ED. But...we've already wheeled the handicapped peoples down front.
JUDY. If you can wheel them in, you can wheel them back

out!
 ED. I should get somebody.
 JUDY. Ed?
 ED. Yes?
 JUDY. *(Leaps up, completely sober)* Gotcha! *(JUDY starts clapping and laughing her head off. It was all an act.)* You should have seen your face! *(Laughs)* Well, I didn't want to disappoint you, pussycat. *(Bows, then starting over.)* Hello. I'm Judy Garland. Liza Minnelli's mother.

(They shake hands.)

 ED. You scared me to death.

(JUDY crosses for a cigarette.)

 JUDY. Oh, that's nothing. Stick around. I usually do two shows a day.

(JUDY takes a cigarette from a case. ED quickly lights it with a nervous hand. She hangs onto his arm.)

 ED. The peoples are looking forward to a great concert.
 JUDY. Yes. *(JUDY takes a puff on her cigarette.)* You know who Paul Henreid is?
 ED. I'm sorry.
 JUDY. Why should you? *(Walking him D.S.)* He was famous for this movie he did with Bette Davis where he lit two cigarettes at once and gave one to her. It was all terribly romantic. Before they invented lung cancer. Anyway, it was 1942 and Hirohito

was kind of winning, so the studios put their stars on a train that toured the country to sell war bonds. The Metro Train, they called it. All the movie stars from M-G-M went—Mickey Rooney, Clark Gable, Ava Gardner...Lucille Ball...you must know Lucy.

ED. Lucy. I love Lucy.

JUDY. Well. We were all there. And at each stop we were trotted out to sing. Or dance. And afterwards people would buy bonds. Well, Paul Henreid was on the train too. And he was the nicest man, very dapper and continental. But he had no act. So I said, "Paul, why don't you do your cigarette bit from 'Now Voyager'?" And he said, "Judy, that's a wahnderfool ahdea." And from then on, everywhere we went he'd light two cigarettes and offer one to a girl in the crowd. Well, suddenly he was a hit. *(Crossing back to chaise)* We used to stop at twenty-thirty towns a day. But after a week we noticed Paul had started to turn a sort of... green. And a few days after that he got sent back to the studio and we found out he had nicotine poisoning. *(Laughs)*

ED. I've seen "The Wizard of Oz" forty-seven times.

JUDY. Huh?

ED. I've seen "The Wizard of Oz" forty-seven times.

JUDY. Are you gay?

ED. No.

JUDY. Of course you're not. *(JUDY sits at chaise.)* Thank you, darling.

(ED follows with an ashtray.)

ED. Is it true the Munchkins were drunk all the time?

JUDY. *(Stubs out her cigarette)* I have done other films, you know. *(Off his look of disappointment)* Yes, they were all drunks.

Every one of them. They kept them all in a big hotel in Culver City, right outside the gates of M-G-M. And every night they'd just get bombed and have their little midget ways with each other. Oh, yes. Every morning they had to send a man with a big butterfly net over to the hotel, and he'd just scoop them all up in the net, load them on the truck and bring them to the set.

ED. Really?

JUDY. Of course. There was one little munchkin in particular who kept asking me out on a date. He was about this tall. And I think he was fifty-three. I was only fifteen years old. And he kept coming after me. Now I didn't want to say, "I can't date you, you're a dwarf." So I said, *(Talking down to the floor, coyly)* "Oh, no thank you. I don't think my mother would approve."

But he didn't care. He said, *(Munchkin voice)* "Bring her along, baby. There's plenty of me to go around." Eventually he fell inside one of the toilets at the studio and we never heard from him again. Oh, yes. No one was prepared for how small these people were.

(JUDY crosses to pour wine, then turns back to ED.)

JUDY. And after this gentleman fell in, the studio had to station people inside the men's and ladies' rooms to help the Munchkins with their...business. How would you like that for an occupation? That would be a good job for Mel Torme.

ED. I met Ray Bolger once.

JUDY. My darling "Scarecrow?" Is that right?

ED. Nice man.

JUDY. Yes, he is. But every movie *(Imitating Ray Bolger leap)* same goddamn dance, no? *(No response from ED)* Never mind.

(JUDY sits S.L.)

ED. Should I send in someone to warm you up?

JUDY. Warm what up? My voice? *(Laughs)* Oh, no, darling. Those days are over. The voice is gone. I just crack my way through for an hour, wave my arms around in that *(Posing dramatically, arms up-stretched)* "Garland way" and hope nobody hits me with an ashtray.

(JUDY stops as her mind drifts. She takes her cigarette and crosses to the dressing table, suddenly distant.)

JUDY. I will need some mashed potatoes, however.

ED. Excuse me?

JUDY. Mashed potatoes. A big bowl. And a spoon. *(No response)* Ed, are you still with us?

ED. This is a concert hall. Where am I going to get mashed potatoes?

JUDY. Copenhagen's a big city. You tell them they're for Judy Garland and she must have mashed potatoes to sing. *(A subtle but deadly warning)* I really can't go on without them, darling. *(Like a little kid)* Sometimes I like them with green beans. I could eat bowls and bowls of them. You're still standing here, Ed.

ED. You're not joking. *(JUDY turns towards him.)* I'll... Omigod.

(ED exits.)

JUDY. I have no intention of going on tonight. *(Pours drink and toasts herself)* Hello. I'm Judy Garland and I'm an alcoholic.

Can you imagine? *(Laughs)* Happy burning. *(Takes a sip)* One of my husbands took me to an AA meeting in Pasadena once. Because he was a drunk! It was so—funny. He got livid because I sat there the entire meeting with a flask of Chivas on my lap. While all those people went on and on about how miserable their lives were. I mean, really. I'll tell you why they were all so miserable. They needed a drink. That would've cheered them right up. Did you ever go to one of those things? You just sit there and sit there and listen to these tortured souls spilling out their troubles like a "who-has-the-most-pathetic-story contest." Ye-Gods.

(JUDY crosses up to the stage monitor.)

JUDY. After an hour of this, I turned to my husband and said, "Get me out of here!" So we headed straight to Romanoff's where we just... got plowed.

(JUDY turns up the stage monitor. We hear:)

JOHNNIE RAY. *(Off; sings)*
IF YOUR HEARTACHE SEEMS TO HANG AROUND TOO LONG...

JUDY. Johnnie Ray. He's marvelous, isn't he?

(JUDY turns the volume up and listens a moment.)

JOHNNIE RAY. *(Off; sings)*
AND YOUR BLUES KEEP GETTING BLUER WITH EACH SONG...

(JUDY turns off the monitor.)

JUDY. We understand each other. Before we were booked for this tour, the only work Johnnie could get was singing in exclusive clubs for a certain type of male clientele. Yes. Very European.

(JUDY crosses D.S.)

JUDY. I've noticed this same particular group of men follows me around everywhere I go. At first I thought it was the same two fellows, and then I realized, "Oh, no. There are thousands of them."

(JUDY crosses S.R. to chaise.)

JUDY. I'm very complimented by it. I must say. I don't understand it, but it's okay with me. I just don't know why they're so fascinated with me. I really don't. But I do love them. I really do. I must. I married a few. A few months ago, I went to see Marlene Dietrich in concert and I noticed those same boys follow her, too. If you've never seen Marlene in concert, it's really fascinating. I don't mean this harshly. However...Marlene isn't one of our better singers. But it doesn't matter—she looks so marvelous. There's not much difference in our ages...anymore. She drops hers down and I can't hide mine, so there you are. Anyway, at a Marlene concert there's always this big overture and you sit there the whole time thinking, "Oh boy she's gonna come out looking great." And she does. It takes them hours to sew her into those dresses. And when she finally comes out, everyone goes *(Gasps)*

THE PROPERTY KNOWN AS GARLAND

"Oh my god she's beautiful." And then that's pretty much the end of the show.

(JUDY crosses to cigarette case at table S.L.)

JUDY. It's all down hill from there. She sings a sad ballad. Then an even sadder ballad. And it's just so sad, you just want to slit your wrists—and I know what I'm talking about. But she does look marvelous.

(JUDY lights her cigarette and stares at herself in the mirror.)

JUDY. I've never had that luxury. I have a very strange body. I'm all legs with this hump thing here and no neck to speak of.

(JUDY sits at the makeup table.)

JUDY. When I sit down at a table opposite a man, all he can see is the top of my head. I haven't any neck at all. But I do have a lovely nose. Don't you think? And unlike Deanna Durbin I have two eyebrows. Deanna was my rival at M-G-M. She sang the classics and I sang jazz. And she had this one thick eyebrow that wouldn't quit. Like a caterpillar across her entire face. She looked positively Hungarian. And when they released her from her contract at Metro, she went to Universal and someone had the good sense to pluck the middle of that one long eyebrow and she became a very big star after that. I have good eyebrows. And a good nose. That's not much to go on. Mr. Louis B. Mayer, who ran Metro-Goldwyn-Mayer... used to refer to me as "the fat one" and "the hunchback." And not behind my back, either. He'd do it right on the set. He'd say, "Do you see this little girl? Look what a star I've turned her into. She used to be a fat little hunchback. Isn't that right, Judy?" And I'd have to answer, "Why, yes, Mr. Mayer. I suppose it is." So I have a bit of an inferiority complex about my looks. When I auditioned for M-G-M I was thirteen years old, and someone asked my mother why I had never been under contract to a studio before, and—

ETHEL GUMM. Take a good at her and figure it out for yourself.

JUDY. So, you see. I'm just a hopeless case. My entire career people have been trying to find ways to camouflage me, or make me pretty. They've put rubber pieces in my nose and capped my crooked teeth and changed my hairline and my color. They stuffed me into canvas body stockings to give me a waist. They put shoulder pads here and here. And when I did my TV show, they even built me a, well, a "rear end." "Ass." I can say "ass," can't I? I'm an adult. They built me an ass. For my tight form-fitting gowns. I may have million dollar legs, but in some trunk somewhere I also have a six hundred dollar ass.

But I do what they tell me. I'm conditioned. *(Taking sip)* Back at Metro, my primary function was to work. As long as I worked, the studio's investment in the "property known as Garland" paid off. If I got fat I couldn't work. And therefore I couldn't get fat.

(JUDY stands next to the dressing table.)

JUDY. They had this clothes dummy at the studio—a great, fat clothes dummy. And they'd make me stand next to it and stare

into the mirror.
STUDIO BOSS. *(Voiceover)* Take a good look at yourself, Judy. Now look at this big, fat, clothes dummy. Which one do you want to be? A big fat dummy, or a star?
YOUNG JUDY. I want to be a star.
STUDIO BOSS. *(Voiceover)* Good girl. From now on, make sure she gets nothing but chicken soup in the commissary.
JUDY. And that's what they gave me. Every day at noon. For thirteen years. Chicken soup. And water. Like a prisoner's menu.

(JUDY picks up a scrapbook.)

JUDY. Now? Even the sight of a chicken? Instant throw-up. Oh. This is my scrapbook. It's not about me. Goodness, no. It's full of just awful news stories. *(Flipping through the pages)* This one's about a girl who was bitten to death by black widow spiders that were living in her beehive hairdo. And this one's my favorite—about a London train wreck where the injured were oh so carefully laid out on an adjoining train track—and killed by the train coming to their rescue. *(Laughs)* Whenever I get really depressed, and need to forget my troubles, I take out this book and say, "Look at this. You think you've got problems!" *(Puts scrapbook away)* It's a chore being Judy Garland. You know how many people pull at me? Demand things of me? Write about me? How many drag queens imitate me? How many people tell my children they know me? They know me. They know Judy Garland. "Poor Judy. She tried to kill herself over four thousand times, you know."

Well, I'm not as helpless as people think! I'm really not. I select all my concert programs, I help design my wardrobe, I supervise my lighting, I help with my musical arrangements. If I didn't know how to do all these things, I'd be pretty dumb after all these years, you know? I'm not in Kansas anymore, folks. But no one wants to hear that. I'll always be Dorothy Gale—just can't get away from "her." Flying over from New York, I can't just sit down. I have to meet the fans. The stewardesses. The pilots.

MAN. *(Voiceover)* Could you sign this for my daughter?
JUDY. Of course, darling.
WOMAN. *(Voiceover)* I loved you in "A Star Is Born."
JUDY. *(Posing)* Thank you, darling.

(Flashes of a camera go off.)

VOICES. *(Voiceover)* Judy/Judy/Over here!

(More flashes)

VOICES. *(Voiceover)* Judy!/One picture?/One more!
JUDY. Thank you, pussycat.

(Flash of a camera)

JUDY. I am so sick of saying thank you! *(Beat)* I've spent years and years and years trying to please people. My mother. Mr. Mayer. You! And no matter how hard I try, I'm constantly written about like I'm some sort of unfit person. Well, I'm not. I'm not! I'm not some sort of a joke. Yet people think I'm either a drunk, or a drug addict or… It's a Goddamned wonder I'm not! But I'm not. I'm just me. I'm loved. I am loved. And fuck anyone who says I'm not. How many deaths do I have to die for you people?

(JUDY crosses for bathroom S.R. She freezes as a framed photo on a wall shelf triggers a memory. She picks up the photo. SFX: The music of a children's singing act from the 1920's sings "The Land of Let's Pretend.")

YOUNG JUDY. *(Voiceover)*
WE'LL LIVE A LIFE OF DREAMS ...
WE'RE DRESSED IN BRIGHT MOONBEAMS
THEY'LL ALL COME TRUE, DEAR
IN THE LAND OF LET'S PRETEND...

JUDY. I made my debut in 1782. Back home in Grand Rapids where I was born. My darling father owned the theater there. And our whole family performed in vaudeville between the movies. "The Gumm Sisters." Jimmie and Suzanne and me. Back then I was Baby Gumm. My mother always picked our songs. The three of us would sing "Dinah"—always "Dinah" and then I'd sing some "ac-tressy" song like "Brother Can You Spare a Dime" or "My Man Bill" with lyrics like "To be on his knee... seems so natural to me." I was four years old. What the hell was I doing on Bill's knee, hm? It was the lousiest act in vaudeville! My mother had no talent whatsoever. She was a hideous wicked woman. I was just a child, but that never mattered. If I was sick or something and didn't want to go onstage, she didn't care. She'd just say, "Get out there and sing or I'll wrap you round the bedpost and break you off short!" Joan Crawford had nothing on her, believe me. We played everywhere. And with everyone. Vaudeville had all sorts of acts. There was this one man who threw up for a living. Yes. His name was Haji Ali. And he threw up on cue. Not an act you wanted to follow, believe me.

There was one man who worked with a singing coyote. He'd drag this skinny mongrel thing out and play the banjo and the coyote would howl. *(Howls)* Well, the Humane Society heard about his act and decided the reason the coyote howled was because the banjo playing was hurting its ears. So they took the coyote away from him. And without his coyote the fellow had no act, so to create a new act, he went to fire eating school. Now, it takes about six months to go through fire eating school, but he had to make a living so he did it in two weeks. We were on the bill with him the night he made his debut and out he came...in flowing robes and everything. And when he got to the point where he was supposed to swallow his first torch, we were in the wings waiting to follow him. And he was so nervous he forgot to put the thick gelatin in his mouth, you know—to keep you from burning to death. And he went "Aaah!" *(Mimes burning her throat with a torch and tossing it)* And he threw the torch, caught the curtain on fire and burned the theater down. And that's when we knew it was time to get out of vaudeville.

(JUDY casually reaches into her makeup kit and takes out a pill bottle. She sees it is empty, she leaves it on the table and crosses to her mink which hangs on the clothes rack U.S.R.)

JUDY. That's when I started performing solo. My sisters didn't enjoy it anyway and to be honest, they just weren't very good.

(Finding the pocket empty, JUDY crosses to the steamer trunk

U.S.L. *The pill bottle there is empty as well.)*

JUDY. I don't talk to them these days. Well, Jimmy, I don't talk to. Suzy's dead.

(She reaches into the pocket of a bathrobe draped over the S.L. chair, where she retrieves a handful of pills.)

JUDY. Killed herself with pills when her husband ran off with a younger woman. Can you imagine? And not like Marilyn Monroe, this was on purpose. *(Pops pill)* Incidentally, I don't believe darling Marilyn meant to harm herself. *(Pops pill)* She simply had too many pills and was completely deserted by her friends at that point. *(Pops pill)* You shouldn't be told you're completely irresponsible and then left alone with too much medication.

(JUDY downs two more pills and drinks some wine to swallow it all down. Then:)

JUDY. Well, you shouldn't! It's too easy to forget. She was a sweet, sweet girl. And, anyway, what was I saying? My sister was a sweet girl too. But if she weren't dead, I still wouldn't talk to her.

(At dressing table, JUDY shakes up her makeup base.)

JUDY. When we lived in Lancaster...California?...if I got too much applause during our shows, my sisters would catch jars full of bees and then after the show, they'd lock me in a room and open the jars. There's not much to do in Lancaster. We moved there when I was two. John Wayne's from Lancaster. And the Duke says, "If you can survive Lancaster, you can survive anything." And he has that right! I had to survive Mother cheating on my darling father with our next-door neighbor. A ghastly, mad haircut-of-a man who eventually left his paralyzed stroke-victim wife for my mother. A match made in hell. I loathed him.

(JUDY sits.)

JUDY. He once stuck the teeth of a rake in the back of a dog that tried breaking into his chicken pen. I'll never forget that sight of that poor dog running down the street dragging that rake as long as I live.
YOUNG JUDY. How can you do this to Daddy?
ETHEL GUMM. *(Voiceover)* Do what to Daddy?
YOUNG JUDY. I know what goes on with you and Mr. Gilmore.
ETHEL GUMM. *(Voiceover)* You don't know as much as you think you do.
YOUNG JUDY. What don't I know?
ETHEL GUMM. *(Voiceover)* Your father is a homosexual, Judy. Why do you think we left Grand Rapids?
JUDY. Imagine telling a five-year-old girl that about her father. There's the real Wicked Witch of the West.

(JUDY opens her base and starts applying.)

JUDY. Two months after I signed with Metro, Daddy went to the hospital with what turned out to be spinal meningitis. Now,

I didn't know how bad it was or I would've spent every second by his side. But Mother didn't tell me.

ETHEL GUMM. *(Voiceover)* You go do your radio job, Judy.

YOUNG JUDY. But Daddy—

ETHEL GUMM. *(Voiceover)* Never mind, Daddy. He'll be fine. We don't want M-G-M to think you're difficult, now, do we?

YOUNG JUDY. But Mama...

ETHEL GUMM. *(Voiceover)* Judy, do you know what it took for me to get you this goddamn studio contract? How many fat, hunchbacked girls do you think they're signing over there? Now get in the car and go sing.

YOUNG JUDY. Yes, Mama.

JUDY. Right before I went on the air, I got a phone call saying they were placing a radio beside Daddy's bed. And right then I knew. Daddy was dying. *(Proudly)* And so I went on. And I sang for Daddy for the last time.

(We hear the radio broadcast of JUDY singing "Zing Went the Strings of My Heart.")

JUDY. *(Voiceover)*
YOUR EYES MADE THE SKY SEEM BLUE AGAIN
WHAT ELSE COULD I DO AGAIN

(JUDY's dialogue resumes over:)

BUT KEEP REPEATING
THROUGH AND THROUGH

I LOVE YOU, LOVE YOU...

JUDY. It was the song I auditioned for M-G-M with. And one of the first songs Daddy ever taught me.

JUDY. *(Voiceover)*
I STILL RECALL THE THRILL
I GUESS I ALWAYS WILL
I HOPE TWILL NEVER DEPART...

(Music fades out.)

JUDY. Daddy died the next morning.

(She brushes the thought aside and closes her base.)

JUDY. That afternoon, a very peculiar thing happened. People started arriving at our house with packages. Gaily wrapped gifts! What we didn't realize is that it was my mother's birthday! And my darling father had arranged a marvelous surprise party for her. So all afternoon guests kept arriving, yelling "Happy Birthday, Ethel!" And then we'd watch them all back out of the house just dying with embarrassment as they heard the news that Daddy was dead. It really got to be quite funny. "Happy Birthday." "Oh, that's terrible!" *(Laughs)* Life's very peculiar. Mother married Mr. Gilmore on November 17, 1939. It was her forty-sixth birthday. And the anniversary of my father's death. That was the most awful thing that ever happened to me. My mother marrying that awful man the same date that my Daddy died. When Mother died she was a fucking riveter at Douglas Aircraft in Long Beach. And that's where she belonged.

(JUDY picks up framed photo of her children.)

JUDY. The only nice thing I will say about my mother is that she taught me not to be cruel to my own children. I should be grateful for that, I suppose.

(JUDY looks at the photo and kisses her children's faces.)

JUDY. Hello, my darlings. You look at those children. I'm so proud of them. Look how they turned out. They're beautiful. They're dynamic. They're loving. And I did that alone. I raised them alone. Because nobody cared about us. Oh, they cared about all the money I brought in because it made them all rich. Not me. Not my children. Well, fuck them. We have each other. And they all three love me. Just the way I love them. After my darling Daddy died, M-G-M more or less adopted me. Metro-Goldwyn-Mayer—where there were "more stars than there are in heaven." And June Allyson worked there, too.

(She takes a drink.)

JUDY. You have no idea the power of the studios back then. They told you how to dress. How to walk. How to speak. What to eat. I think they even taught Rin Tin Tin how to bark. Louis B. Mayer was the most powerful man in Hollywood. When Mother wanted to discipline me all she had to say was: "I'll tell Mr. Mayer." And that worked, believe me. If Mr. Mayer didn't like your behavior he'd fine you, he'd sell you like cattle, he'd put you in a sanitarium and give you electric shock treatments, or even worse—he'd make you work with Busby Berkeley! Ava Gardner used to say we were the only merchandise that got to leave the store at night. But back then, the word of Louis B. was the law. He was a good picture maker. He made great pictures. Our meetings in his office always ended with the same routine.

STUDIO BOSS. Judy, you little hunchback...

JUDY. He always called me a hunchback.

STUDIO BOSS. Judy, you little hunchback, you sing from the heart.

JUDY. And then he'd stick his hand on my breast to show me where my heart was. Like I didn't know. I often thought, "Gee, I'm damn lucky I don't sing from another part of my anatomy." But he was a good man. He made me a star. Or what is it they call me now? A living legend. That's what I'm supposed to be, right? A living legend. Last year I was sleeping on the couch of a fan, after the I.R.S. took everything I owned. My sheet music. My arrangements, my gowns. I sang for a hundred bucks a night—cash—at some little lesbian bar in the Village. There's your living legend for you.

Barely living. I think I've made over ten million dollars in my lifetime. And where is it? Where did it all go? Where's my money? *(Looks under things)* Do you have it? My children don't have it. And I sure as hell don't have it. But my mother sure got her share, though. And Metro-Goldwyn-Mayer too. I'll tell you what M-G-M stands for. My Goddamn Money. "Living legend" my six hundred dollar ass. Maybe I'd believe it, too, if M-G-M hadn't destroyed my self-confidence, who knows? They did. They did it to all of us. Mickey Rooney, Lana Turner, myself, Deena Durbin, Freddie Bartholomew. Have you seen how we all turned out? We're all a bit peculiar. All a bit ticky and kooky. Look at Elizabeth Taylor!

Oh, that was just rude. It's not nice to speak ill of the dead, am I right? Is she still alive? Oh. Well, in that case...she's nuts! But it's not her fault. M-G-M did that to us. They took away all our self-worth. Because if we knew we had value, we'd ask for more money, you see? We never even saw our fan mail. We had no idea we were famous at all—until Mickey Rooney and I were shipped off to do seven shows a day at all the Loew's Theaters... to promote the pictures. And we knew something was up—when we saw women hurling themselves at Mickey's limousine. But the studio did their best to hide it all from us. So there's only one place I've ever felt loved. Not at home. Not at the studio. In front of audiences who let me sing for them. And it's been that way since I was two. I just played some dates in London. And I did my best. But I'm tired. I'm very tired these days. And I just want to stop. But they won't let me. Because I need money. So here we are. But at the Town and Country, Talk of the Town or whatever the place was called, I was late. A little late. For me. And when I walked out on that stage to sing, people threw cigarettes at me.

(Overlapping voices:)

DRUNK #1. *(Voiceover)* Go back to Hollywood!
DRUNK #2. *(Voiceover)* Who do you think you are?!
DRUNK #3. *(Voiceover)* Go home! You old drunk!
JUDY. I did my best. I'm only one person. What do you want from me? I've spent my whole life entertaining you people. I've pleased every one of you, you sons of bitches. And you hit me with cigarettes? You hit me with ashtrays? Well, fuck you.

Fuck you all, you sons of bitches!

(JUDY violently knocks things from the makeup table onto the floor. ED enters with a brown paper bag.)

    ED. Miss Garland. There isn't a bowl of mashed potatoes in all of Copenhagen. I got you some chips potato.
    JUDY. Well, fine. Then you'll have to go tell the producers.
    ED. Excuse me?

(JUDY heads for her mink.)

    JUDY. I was so looking forward to doing a good show, too. Would you have them send my car, darling?
    ED. Looking forward? What are you...but...you cannot...
    JUDY. *(Turning on him)* I did my best. You tell the producers I was here. I was willing. I was on time! And they'll have to pay me anyway. Makes no difference to me. I'm still getting my money.

(JUDY heads back for her mink.)

    ED. No. Please. Wait a minute.
    JUDY. *(Putting on mink.)* You wait a minute. I just don't know what the problem is.
    ED. If we'd known you needed potatoes we would have made arrangements. When we spoke with your manager we were told to supply you with bottles of Blue Nun, no one said anything about potatoes.
    JUDY. Well, then what can I do? You leave me no choice.

(JUDY heads for the dressing room door. ED blocks her exit.)

ED. Wait, please. Let's not "blow this" over a bowl of potatoes.
JUDY. Blow this? Whaddya mean, blow this? Who's blowing it, Buster? Me?
ED. I...
JUDY. Everything's always my fault. All my fucking life.
ED. I don't know what...it's nine o'clock at night. What can I do?
JUDY. How would I know what you can do? I never met you before. But if you don't care enough—
ED. I...
JUDY. IF YOU DON'T CARE ENOUGH, then let the lady off the hook and get me my car.
ED. What happened here?
JUDY. You tell me.
ED. I don't know.
JUDY. Well, if you don't know, I certainly can't tell you. Why should this be any different? I called M-G-M last week to get my husband a copy of "Meet Me in St. Louis" because he'd never seen it before, and the girl on the phone didn't even know who I was, after all the money I made for those bastards. I made those bastards over one hundred million dollars in my time. Didn't even know who I was. Then the capper? After apologizing up and down, they send me some Irene Dunne movie. *(Beside herself in tears)* Nobody cares about me anymore! How am I supposed to go on?

(A beat. ED gently offers her the Kleenex box from the dressing

table.)

ED. I will get you some mashed potatoes, Miss Garland. Please continue to get dressed.
JUDY. *(Taking Kleenex)* Thank you, pussycat.

(ED replaces the box and exits. JUDY turns to the audience, dropping any hint of hysteria.)

JUDY. He's a nice boy. *(Tossing Kleenex)* You have no idea what it's like for me before I go onstage. It's terrifying. Paralyzing. And exhilarating. It's sort of a combination of feeling like Queen Victoria and an absolute ass. I should just hire one of those boys to come out and imitate me and see if anyone knows the difference.

(JUDY picks up the beaded bag.)

JUDY. There's a marvelous young man named Jim Bailey who does me better than me. I went to see him in concert one night, and at the intermission I had a marvelous idea. So I went backstage, and we switched costumes and then I went on and did Act Two. Doing my best Judy Garland—flailing my arms, stammering, forgetting where I was in the program, and belting out those Garland march songs...and oh, goodness, it was hard work.

(JUDY removes her coat, and continues getting ready.)

JUDY. And Jim sat out in the audience, dressed as me—

just…sitting there—and he was laughing up a storm—because no one knew the difference!

Afterwards, a charming little old woman went up to Jim, pointed at the stage, and said, "He's no you!" *(Reacts)* I do so prefer the concerts to the movies. I love the immediate response. At Metro I waited sixteen years for someone to say "Good job, Judy." And you know something? In sixteen years I never heard it once.

(JUDY pours more wine.)

JUDY. Not that I haven't had my share of mishaps in the concerts. It wouldn't be very Garland without the mishaps, would it? I played the Greek Theatre in Hollywood, which is an open air theater. And there are an awful lot of insects involved because the lights attract all kinds of moths. Well, back then at the end of my act, I'd sit on the edge of the stage with my feet hanging over the footlights, and I'd sing "Over the Rainbow." Now "Over the Rainbow" takes, well, a big breath to sing, and that night as I breathed in, a moth flew in my mouth. Now in the middle of "Get Happy' you can go *(Makes spitting noise)* "Hoch-tu," but not in the middle of "Over the Rainbow." It just would have ruined the whole evening. And so I parked that little moth in my cheek for a whole chorus and a half. I had a faster vibrato than ever that night.

And when the lights went down and came back up, all people could see was me going, "Hoch-tu" and stamping my foot. *(Demonstrates)* Sort of the same act Marlene Dietrich does.

(JUDY crosses to the rack for a costume and pulls a gold bro-

cade pantsuit off the clothes rack.)

JUDY. *(Re: pantsuit)* "The Valley of the Dolls." What a piece of shit. They asked me to make one of my many "comebacks" in that terrible, dirty picture. My daughter Liza told me not to do it.

(JUDY tosses the costume over the back of the chaise.)

JUDY. She said they were making fun of me with the role of that pill-popping actress. But—story of my life—I needed the money. They didn't want me for that role, anyway. That was for Patty Duke. Little Helen Keller was playing me, I suppose. And I was supposed to be playing Ethel Merman. And I'm about as much like Ethel Merman as Peter Allen. Less! So there I am on the set in my costume—this costume—and the director is just... yelling at me.
DIRECTOR. *(Voiceover)* Meaner, Judy. Just a little meaner.
JUDY. Huh?
DIRECTOR. *(Voiceover)* Meaner. I need you meaner.
JUDY. What does that even mean—"be meaner"?
DIRECTOR *(Voiceover)* You don't know what the word "meaner" means?
JUDY. I know what the word means. I know all sorts of words, darling. Like, let's see... "incompetent." That's a good word. And "unprepared," that's another one. And "out of his league." No, sorry. That's four words. Let's get something straight. I take great pride in my work. And I do not want to be seen as a harridan on the screen. And my fans don't want to see me that way either. Got it, buster? George Cukor. There's a direc-

tor. Stanley Kramer who directed me in "Judgment at Nuremberg." I would play a leper on Molokai for that man, but you, sir, are no director. That mean enough for you? *(To audience)* So I walked out. And they replaced me with that great songstress Miss Susan Hayward. A drunk.

(JUDY holds up the "Valley" pantsuit.)

JUDY. But I kept the costume. I wonder what Susan's wearing tonight. Oh, the hell with it.

(JUDY drops the gold pantsuit and grabs the red sleeveless pantsuit from the rack instead. She crosses behind the changing screen.)

JUDY. I'll go behind here. We wouldn't want anything too gay to happen, now would we?

(She changes into the red costume during the following.)

JUDY. Another quick Marlene Dietrich story. I was in Paris with Noel Coward and some friends and we were just sitting around and Marlene had been doing a tour for many months, and she came in with a great big record. A great big record. Bigger than a twelve inch.

And she said, "Oh, darling, Would anyone wike to hear my wecord? So we said "Sure we'd wove to hear your wecord." We couldn't say "No we don't want to hear your wecord." So she put the record on. And it was just... applause. Really. There'd be a big burst of applause and she'd say, "That's Frankfurt." And then there'd be a big "Hurrah" and she's say, "That's Berlin." But not one note of music.

She didn't sing. There was no orchestra. Just applause. It was insane. And Noel turned to me and said, "I hope there isn't another side to this wecord." And there was!'

(JUDY emerges from behind the screen, attaching a red feather-trimmed skirt around the pantsuit.)

JUDY. There. Not bad for forty-six. Amazing what you can do with putty and string these days. I designed this myself, you know. Yes. *(Demonstrates)* I can detach the skirt and wear it as a cape too—for...whenever I want to look like Orson Welles. Orson was a neighbor of mine. And he'd always come by unannounced at 3 o'clock in the morning wearing a cape. And he'd walk right past me into my living room reciting lines from "MacBeth." And I'd have to say, "Out! Out, Damn Orson!" He makes me laugh. My favorite Orson story concerns a play he opened in Washington. Now, Orson is a great director, obviously—"Citizen Kane" and...that other one. And I think he got a few more in there, too. Well, when he started out in the theater, he did all sorts of weird, wonderful plays. He used platforms that came up out of no where, and revolving stages, and all sorts of mechanical things that hadn't been done on the stage before. And he was doing a very elaborate play.

I think it was a Shakespearean play. In fact, I think it was a combination of three Shakespearean plays. And at one point Orson had fifty soldiers in Crusade outfits, you know, with helmets and big boots, march out onto the stage with bows and arrows...and they pulled their bows and arrows and shot the arrows into the wings where there was a big board to, you know, catch them all.

And it went all right during rehearsal. And then they opened in Washington. And it was all very formal with all sorts of senators in black ties and ladies in...a lot of pearls and hair spray... and these fifty soldiers came marching out and they stood and pulled their bows and arrows. And just as they pulled their bows and arrows somebody pushed the button to turn the revolving stage, and fifty arrows went straight into the audience. People were running for their lives. Senators were screaming, "Let's get out of here!" Orson didn't even care. You see, most of them were Republicans.

(JUDY gets her shoes from the wardrobe trunk.)

JUDY. Orson's a big man, you know. But about seven years ago, I weighed more than he does. Yes. I was a hundred and eighty-five pounds. And I'm barely five feet tall. Anyway, I went to England to rest. I got bored resting in America all the time. And they had a great big press reception for me. We were all put into a sort of un-air conditioned room in the middle of London and everyone was asking rude questions the way the English press always does.

REPORTER #1. *(Voiceover)* Why did you lose all your money?

REPORTER #2. *(Voiceover)* Which number husband is this one?

REPORTER #3. *(Voiceover)* How many times have you tried to kill yourself?

JUDY. You try to rise above this. You really want to give

them a shot in the head, but you don't. You just say, *(As gracious star)* "Thank you. It's so nice to be back in London."

REPORTER #4. *(Voiceover)* Yeah, yeah, yeah. So, how many abortions have you had?

JUDY. Well, there was one woman from the press. Sort of nice looking and friendly and she came over and said, "You look marvelous." Now, mind you, I didn't. I didn't at all. I looked awful. I was obese. That's O Henry's second cousin. But she was so sweet to me, kept saying, "You look marvelous. You look marvelous. What are you doing for yourself? Marvelous." So I thought, "I'm sticking with you, sister." And I hung around her the whole night. The next day I pick up the paper and I see she has a great big four column article. And in big bold letters, it says: "Judy Garland Arrives in London. She's not chubby. She's not plump. She's FAT!"

(JUDY gets her wine.)

JUDY. It made me yearn for the M-G-M days when we never saw newspapers. They worked us six days a week from eight in the morning until three in the morning—for fifteen straight years. You'd finish one picture on Saturday and start your next picture on Monday. It was a schedule no one should've had to endure. Least of all a thirteen-year-old girl. And I had no one to fight for me. My darling father was gone. My mother did as she was told. *(Sips)* She only stood up for me one time. I was working with Busby Berkeley on "Strike Up the Band." I was beyond exhaustion. Buzz would work you until two in the morning if he felt like it. And he'd save the close-ups for last. A horrible, horrible man. He was a perfectionist and a drunk. If he didn't like what he saw while you were filming he'd scream at you to Open your eyes! "Open your eyes! I want to see eyes!" So I'd... *(Bugs her eyes out)* You go look at that picture. I look like Eddie Cantor with my eyes popping out like that. Sometime later, after I'd already been fired from M-G-M, Mr. Berkeley's mother died and he went a bit nuts. He took a broken bottle and slashed his throat—and not like me, he really slashed it! They stuck him in a psychiatric ward at Los Angeles General—in a dirty old strait jacket. And he was such a miserable man...nobody cared: I'm sure that opened his eyes!

(JUDY sits and does her powder.)

JUDY. Anyway, back before his strait-jacket days, we were filming "Strike Up the Band" and I just couldn't go on. It was inhumane the way he treated his stars. And I take pride in my work. I have to be my best in front of a camera. And sometimes I don't feel my best. That's when they started giving me pills to keep me awake, and pills to go to sleep. And diet pills. They gave them to everybody. To keep us going, you know? Everyone thinks it's such a "Garland" thing, but every actor in Hollywood took them—even Rin Tin Tin. Well, the pills made me sick. And so I started missing work. So my mother went to Mr. Mayer and demanded, demanded! That I be allowed to go home after eight hours each day. Mr. Mayer listened too. Then he had her banned from the studio for six months, until she learned to mind her own business and keep her mouth shut. She never contradicted him ever, ever again.

(JUDY puts on a necklace, looking at herself in the mirror.)

JUDY. Like when I married David Rose. The composer? David was a very strange fellow. He used to ride these little trains. Little toy trains. In endless circles around our backyard. After a frantic day at the studio, he'd come home and put on a conductor's cap and sit in his goddamn train and ride the rails. I did it too. But I started feeling sort of silly. I thought when I got married I'd come home and have smart dinner parties and make love and go out dancing—but—he rode trains in circles. Well, one day I found out I was pregnant. All day I waited in the house for David to finish his train ride so I could tell him the news, but before I got to him, Mother took him upstairs. A short while later she came down alone.

ETHEL GUMM. *(Voiceover)* Now Judy, you understand. This is impossible. This baby. You cannot have it.

YOUNG JUDY. Why not? It's mine. And I want it.

ETHEL GUMM. *(Voiceover)* You don't seem to understand. Mr. Mayer thinks it's a bad idea. And I do, too. Baby Gumm does not have babies! You'll have more at the right time.

YOUNG JUDY. It's my life!

ETHEL GUMM. *(Voiceover)* Not as long as you work for M-G-M, it isn't.

YOUNG JUDY. David won't let you do this. *(Rises and calls off)* David! David?

(A beat)

JUDY. David never came down. The next day I sat between David and my Mother and they drove me to the outskirts of Los Angeles to, how do they say it, "take care of it." And shortly after, David…rode the next train out of town.

THE PROPERTY KNOWN AS GARLAND 39

(JUDY sits and stares at herself in the mirror.)

JUDY. Years later I was pregnant with my daughter Liza and I was still haunted by that earlier time. So much so that I went to my mother and asked her permission—her permission! Luckily, by then I was married to Mr. Vincente Minnelli and had made adult pictures like "The Clock" and "Meet Me in St. Louis."

ETHEL GUMM. *(Voiceover)* Yes, Judy—you can have a baby—this time.

JUDY. That's a nice mother, isn't it? That's a fine upstanding, caring woman. Maybe I fulfilled Mother's ambitions. I really don't know. I don't give it any thought.

(JUDY puts on bracelet. ED returns.)

ED. Okay, they're coming!
JUDY. What?

(JUDY puts on earring during the following.)

ED. They're coming. I went out into the streets and started knocking on doors. A lady in an apartment ten streets away has agreed to make you mashed potatoes. I sounded like a crazy person. I'm surprised they didn't call the police. But she must have seen my eyes of desperation, and well, she's making the potatoes. I have someone waiting there to drive them over here. They should be here in, I don't know...three minutes. All right?

JUDY. Thank you, Ed. You're so good to me.
ED. Yes, Ma'am. Ten minutes Miss Garland.
JUDY. That's fine. *(Exiting into restroom.)* Who's bringing

the green beans?

ED. Potatoes. You mean potatoes.

JUDY. *(Entering, with lipstick in hand)* No, darling. I know about the potatoes. I'm talking about the green beans.

ED. The green beans.

JUDY. I eat them mixed together. Didn't we discuss this, Ed?

(ED stares and then simply exits.)

JUDY. She never watched out for me, my mother. Never. After sixteen years and no time off, I was at the end of my rope. I was holding on by a thread, mind you. And they put me into another picture... "Annie Get Your Gun." Directed by that Nazi bastard—Busby Berkeley! And this monster treated me the same at twenty-eight as when I was fifteen. That son of a bitch just ripped me to ribbons. Just to get out of work one day, I slashed my wrists. Not deep. Not in true Busby Berkeley fashion. But enough. It was all very hysterical. There was blood everywhere. And people were screaming. But I did get the day off! *(Beat)* And then for no Goddamn reason at all, they fired me. After all the money I made those sons of bitches. Betty Hutton took my part in "Annie Get Your Gun." Good for her. She cooks for priests now. So it all worked out, I suppose. She's a drunk, you know.

(JUDY gets into her shoes.)

JUDY. I hate shoes. Hate them. I think the Marquis De Sade invented these things, don't you? *(Clicks them)* There's no place like home. There's no place like home. Thank God!

THE PROPERTY KNOWN AS GARLAND

Is it any wonder I ended up in a "nuthouse"? My very first—you always remember your first, don't you?—my very first nuthouse was Las Campanas, a sanitarium somewhere outside beautiful downtown Compton. They put me in my own little bungalow *(Framing her face with her hands, a la "A Star Is Born")* —I was a movie star, after all—right next to what they called "the violent ward" where I got to hear all sorts of disturbing "Snake Pit" screaming. Yes.

(JUDY returns to the dressing table.)

JUDY. And it was a very expensive place. I saw a man wearing this beautiful tooled leather belt. And I said, "Oh, that's a marvelous belt." He said, "Thank you. I made it in the therapy room. And it only cost me $182,000." The entire time I was in there, my mother only called me once.

ETHEL GUMM. *(Voiceover)* There's something wrong with your brain, do you know that?

(SFX: Hang-up and dial tone.)

JUDY. Wicked old witch. My mother died right after my daughter Lorna was born. But I was done with her by then. So I gave the order to the hospital not to let her in. And I still don't give a damn. It took me long enough to get a backbone. But by God, I have one now. Fucking riveter. Good riddance. *(Beat)* Good riddance to those hospitals, too. Mr. Mayer came to visit me in the last one and told me not to worry—the studio would pay the bills for all the sanitariums they'd "forced" me into all those years. And right then and there he called his bosses in New

York to get approval and...I'll never forget it. He hung up the phone—his face white as a sheet.

STUDIO BOSS. *(Voiceover)* The New York office suggests you go to a charity hospital. They said...we're not in the money-lending business.

JUDY. "There's no business like show business" all right. Mr. Mayer? Are you all right?

STUDIO BOSS. *(Voiceover)* Don't you see, Judy? If they'll do this to you, they'll do this to me, too.

JUDY. He was right. A year later M-G-M fired the great Louis B. Mayer. And they haven't made a decent picture since! Sons of bitches.

(JUDY applies her blush during the following.)

JUDY. Mr. Mayer paid my hospital bills himself, by the way. Out of his own pocket. After all, I did sing from the heart. *(Grabs her own breast)* One month later, Bing Crosby called me—bless him. My phone hadn't rung at all. Let me say, there's nothing worse in Hollywood than "having been" a movie star. "Judy," he said, "I know how busy you are." Busy? "But...could I get you to guest on my radio show?" That moment my whole world changed. I needed that job more than I needed money. You can always borrow money. You can't borrow a job. You can't borrow the chance to put faith back in yourself. Somebody has to have faith in you first. Well, Bing had faith in me. And thank God, I didn't let him down. That night, as I started to sing, an even more powerful sound came out of me than I ever had before. I wasn't singing for Metro, or for Mama anymore. I was singing for me. I've had that voice ever since. You can hear it on the Carnegie Hall album.

(JUDY rises, crosses to trunk. She remembers the night, as we hear "Swanee" as she sang it at Carnegie Hall. The song ends. The applause echoes in her mind.)

JUDY. *(Voiceover)*
YOUR WANDERING CHILD
WILL WANDER NO MORE.
WHEN I GET TO THAT SWANEE SHORE.

JUDY. Now, that was a good wecord. I knocked Mr. Elvis Presley off the charts with that album, you know. Yes. Sid tried getting Elvis for one of my TV specials. Wouldn't that have been interesting? "Suspicious Minds" at CBS prevailed, however, and we wound up going with Topo Gigio or someone. "Sid" is Sid Luft, by the way. My ex-husband. A lot's been said about Sid Luft. By me. Let me just say this. Sid took care of me like no one else. Carnegie Hall and my Grammy Award? Sid Luft. The Palace Theatre? Sid Luft. My TV show? Sid Luft. "A Star Is Born?" Sid Luft. And who paid for it all? Judy Garland. *(Crossing left)* "A Star Is Born." That was a good picture. I earned that Oscar nomination, let me tell you. My entire life's work went into that film.

I did everything in that picture, except ride upside down on Francis the Talking Mule.

I had just given birth to my Joey, my darling son, and I was still recovering in the hospital. All of a sudden three great big men came into my room, in the maternity ward, carrying television sets. *(Gesturing towards window)* Then up goes the Venetian blind and I see a big three-story tower out-side the hospital that they'd obviously been constructing for days.

I said, "What's this for?" And they said, *(As gruff worker)* "You're going to get the Academy Award tonight and we've got to put these sets in here so you can thank Bob Hope live on television when you win it." *(Crossing to chaise)* And I think, "I must have won. Otherwise, they wouldn't go to all this trouble!" So they put a microphone wire up my ass and down through my nightie and cover me up to here with feathers. My poor nurse is told she has to operate the Venetian blind. And she's just frozen with terror, because she doesn't know "show biz," you know? *(Sits)* So, there I am leaning against my pillow covered in feathers with a wire up my ass trying to look oh-so glamorous, with my terrified nurse ready at the Venetian blind. And then Bob Hope opens that envelope and says, "And the winner is...Grace Kelly in 'The Country Girl!'" And I went, "Whaat?"

And the next moment I look up, everyone's gone. *(Rising, crossing left)* In about three seconds, they've torn down the tower. They've ripped out the wires...out go the television sets. And nobody even said good night. They were just so mad at me! But I got something better than any award— *(Kisses photo of her son)* my son Joey. So...let the Princess keep her fucking Oscar.

(JUDY crosses back to the dressing table for her drink.)

JUDY. Drunk. *(Drinks)* But I deserved it. I deserved it! It's very hard to put your heart and your soul into something and then have your face slapped. I deserved it. What do you do after you give everything there is to give and it's not good enough? Well, I just fell apart. I staggered along in a nightmare for two years. A virtual automaton. I played some big concert dates in 1958 and 1959 and don't remember a single one of them. *(Drinks)* And then my liver started to swell up. Four times its size. Acute hepatitis—not very cute if you ask me. The doctor said I only had a few months to live. I'd never sing again. And if I was to be cured at all, I could never ever touch hard liquor. *(Sips)* Well, what did they know? I lived. And I'm still singing. The only bad part was I had to say goodbye to vodka and learn to drink Blue Nun. Cheers.

(JUDY toasts the audience and drinks. She sees a framed photo of Jack Kennedy on the dressing table and toasts that.)

JUDY. Cheers, Jack.

(JUDY picks up photo.)

JUDY. Jack Kennedy was my friend. I think he was the greatest man I ever knew. I loved him dearly. Whenever he had a bad day at the White House he'd call me up and I'd sing him "Over the Rainbow" over the phone. He liked that. When he was murdered...I don't like the word "assassinate." It trivializes everything, doesn't it? This was a person. A man. A great man. And he was murdered. In tribute, I planned a show of patriotic songs for my television program. But CBS sent word down from on high— "No tributes." They just refused to let me do it. And I said, "You're not telling me I can't do this. I knew him! He was my friend! I'm doing it!"

(JUDY sits.)

JUDY. So I wait a month and sneak in "The Battle Hymn of the Republic" at the close of my show.

(JUDY brushes her hair.)

JUDY. It's supposed to be a secret, but word leaks out and Mr. Hunt Stromberg Jr. shows up. Hunt Stromberg Jr. was the VP from CBS. A hundred and thirty years old. And he looked it. His father was at M-G-M when they still made silent movies—and he hated my guts. And now the son was in charge of my TV show. And he says, "Absolutely no tributes. The show won't air until January and the country will have forgotten Kennedy by then anyway." *(Rising)* "You ghoul, I'm singing it. What are you going to do, cancel my show?" *(Beat)* You'll notice I'm not on television anymore.

(JUDY crosses to chair with wine.)

JUDY. No one was there for me at our final taping. No one's ever there at the end. They all walk away from me. Walk away backwards. And smiling. My managers were in New York for the opening of "Funny Girl" with their new client Miss Barbra Streisand. Out with the old... *(Drinks)* So I was alone. I had counted on the TV show to get me out of all the financial messes I was in, so I was bubbling at the brim with all sorts of emotions. And as I started to sing the first number, I just lost it. I staggered off the stage and barricaded myself in the dressing room and...just... sobbed.

In between tears, I look over and...see an orchid on my dressing table. An orchid. I look at the card and realize it's from

Mr. Hunt Stromberg Jr. And it reads, "You're THROUGH—GET OUT!"

(She laughs her head off.)

JUDY. What have I learned from all this? *(Thinks, then:)* Hell if I know. I'm just lucky I'm still here, I guess. All in all, I'm a very lucky woman. *(Rising)* I've got my children. I have my audiences. And they don't desert me. Never! They're my only constant. And for once in my life I'm finally with a man who loves me. Me. Not my voice—because it's gone. Not my money—because I didn't have any when I met him, and I don't have any now. He loves ME. Whether I sing or dance or whether I don't. And he thinks I'm pretty. *(Finishes lipstick, into mirror)* Me. Pretty. You hear that, Mama? When we get back to the States my lovely husband is going to set up a chain of movie theaters: The Judy Garland Theaters, they're going to call them. And I'll finally be set for life. That will truly be the property known as Garland, won't it?

(JUDY puts makeup back into makeup kit.)

JUDY. After all the years of being taken. Robbed. Used. I'll be disgustingly rich. And I can just...stop! A million dollars for just using my name. Mickey says they'll be more famous than Grauman's Chinese Theater. And we can grow old together. I'll never have to sing again unless I want to. How about that?

(ED enters with a bowl of mashed potatoes, a bowl of green beans, and a wooden spoon.. He's out of breath. Offstage,

we hear the audience anxiously awaiting the show.)

ED. I made it. I made it. I can't breathe. Here you go.

JUDY. Where the hell have you been? Start the overture, pussycat. They're waiting!

ED. Uh...don't you need to eat first?

JUDY. I never eat before a show, darling. How am I supposed to sing with blobs of potatoes in my throat?

(JUDY scrapes the potatoes into the trashcan.)

ED. But...

(She quickly ushers ED out the door.)

JUDY. Let's go, Ed! "You never know when it's going to be your last one," so I say "always go out strong!"

ED. Yes, Ma'am.

JUDY. Go! Go! Go!

(ED exits. The door is left open. JUDY watches from the wings a beat then rushes to finish up. We hear strains of "Over the Rainbow" within the overture. At the sound of "Rainbow" she stops to listen, frozen with terror. The audience cheers and applauds wildly at the recognition. JUDY smiles, relieved.)

JUDY. I've always taken the "Wizard of Oz" very seriously, you know. I believe in the idea of the rainbow. And I've spent my entire life trying to get over it. Well, I'll tell you something. I think I've finally made it! Recently, one of those English reporters asked me if I'd do it all over again. "You bet your life, Buster. With all the same mistakes, too." I was put on this earth to give. To give my heart and soul to my audiences. I can't do any less. I really can't. I never will. This same idiot said people only come to my shows now to see me fail. Can you believe that? To see me fail? I'll tell you why people come to see me. They come to see me succeed!

(She hears applause as the overture continues.)

JUDY. You'll never know this kind of love, Mama. It's the one thing you couldn't take from me. *(Motions off)* That's mine! They love me. Hunchback and crooked teeth and insecurities all. And that love is mine! Alone! I love them! And I need them! But you know something? They need me too!

(The overture swells. On the final drum roll, JUDY enters the stage. The offstage audience roars.)

CURTAIN

COSTUMES

JUDY GARLAND

Black clam-diggers
Pink-striped tailored shirt (oversized)
Black leather slip on (60's, low heel)

ED

Blue 60's oxford shirt
Tie (thin, 1960's)
Tie bar
Tweed sports coat with pockets, small lapels
Trousers, no pleat, tapered leg, sharkskin plaid
Black penny loafers
   Into:
Navy wool peacoat
Woolen scarf and hat

PRE-SET ON STAGE

<u>On clothing rack:</u>
"Valley of the Dolls" suit: gold/copper paisley brocade with beading (prop/not worn)
White beaded brocade suit with red scarf (prop/not worn)
Black or brown mink, 3/4 length with pockets and collar (late 60's)
Red silk pantsuit with side zip (worn)

Matching silk chiffon paneled skirt on waistband with dyed-to-match ostrich feather trim (worn)

<u>In trunk:</u>
Rhinestone earrings
Rhinestone/pearl necklace and bracelet
Rhinestone and pearl ring
Period red heels, dyed to match pantsuit

PROPERTY LIST

Ashtray
Beaded purse
Blue Nun bottle (3)
Blush
Brown bag
Cigarettes (herbal) (3 per show)
Cigarette case (gold)
Clipboard
Eyeliner pencil
Yellow roses
Framed photo: The Gumm Sisters
Framed Photo: JFK
Framed Photo: Judy Garland and Children
Gold brocade pantsuit ("Valley of the Dolls")
Green beans
Hand mirror
Hairbrush
Jewelry case
Kleenex
Lighter fluid
Lipstick
Liquid base
Makeup brush
Makeup sponge
Mashed potatoes
Pearl bracelet
Pearl earrings
Pearl necklace
Pearl ring

THE PROPERTY KNOWN AS GARLAND

Pencil
Pill bottle (2)
Pocket watch
Powder & puff
Ring box
Robe
Salem box
Sand
Scrapbook of horrible news stories
Charts (handwritten sheet music)
Suitcase
Tic Tacs (red) (5 nightly)
Trashcan
Trunk
White brocade pantsuit with green sequins
White cranberry or grape juice (to water down)
Wine glass (plus spare)
Wooden bowl, 6" diameter
Wooden bowl, 10" diameter
Wooden hangers (5)
Wooden spoon
Zippo lighter (3 plus spares)

Furniture
Chaise (4 1/2' X 2')
Changing screen
Clothes rack
Club chair
Dressing table
Chair
Side table

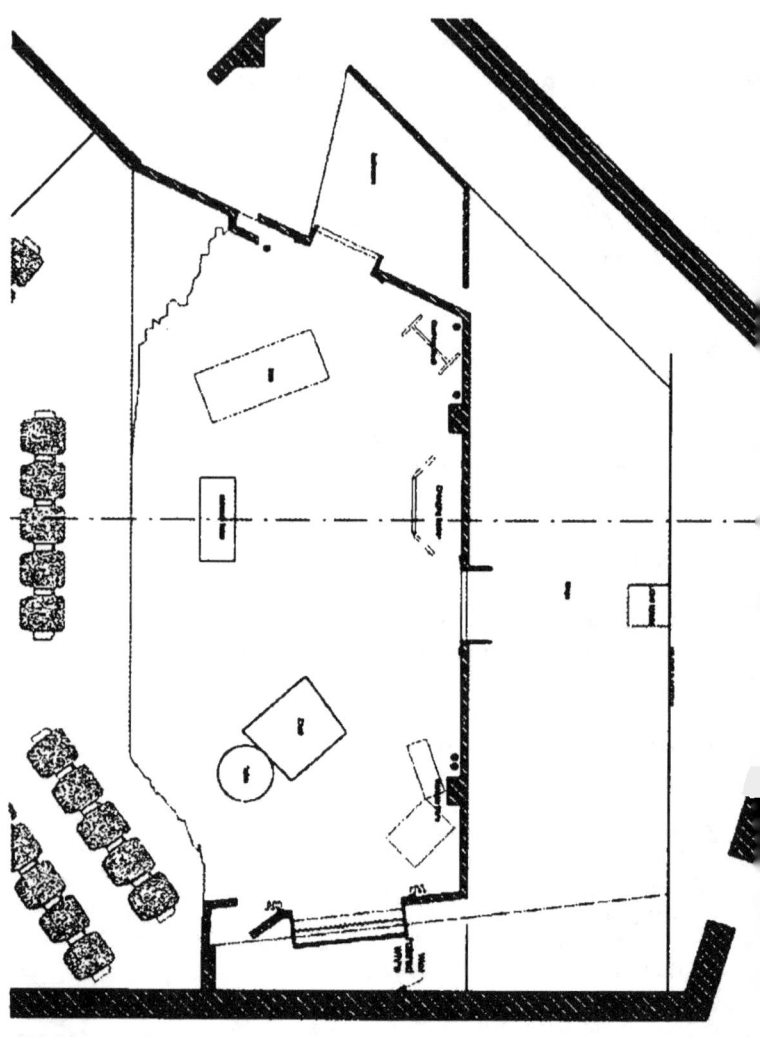

SET DESIGN

www.ingramcontent.com/pod-product-compliance
Lightning Source LLC
Chambersburg PA
CBHW072022290426
44109CB00018B/2312